Poetic Perspectives on Faith and Healing

Copyright © 2010, 2016 by Ameedah Diaab Abdullah

All Rights Reserved. No part of this book may be reproduced in any form or by any means, electronic or mechanical, including photocopying without written permission of the author.

All inquiries and copy requests should be addressed to:

Ameedah Diaab Abdullah
Felicitous Fonts, Inc.
3378 Greenbriar Parkway S.W., Suite 5105
Atlanta, Georgia
30331

Also by the author: Tell Me About Al Islam,
A Primer For Preschoolers, 1996

ISBN 978-0-692-63010-5

Library of Congress on file

1st Publication by Rathsi Publishing, 2010
2nd Publication by Felicitous Fonts, Inc., 2016
Printed in the United States of America

Suratul Iklas
(Purity of Faith)

Say: He is Allah, The One, Allah,
The Absolute, Eternal,
He begets not, nor is He begotten,
And there is none like unto Him.

Chapter 112 Holy Quran

Dedicated to all "believing people"
who are seeking mental and spiritual restoration
with the Creator's permission.

With God's Name,

The Merciful Benefactor, The Merciful Redeemer

Acknowledgments

All praise belongs to the Almighty Creator, whom I choose to call Allah, (SWT) highly glorified is He. I bear witness that He is the Greatest. Greater than any challenge that one might encounter.

I am grateful that He granted the experiences that enabled me to become a survivor and for placing numerous friends and supporters in my path on my quest to know Him. Through His word, in the Bible and Quran, I was able to learn about many of the prophets that set the examples of righteous living. Prophet Muhammad, (PBUH), the final messenger, set the perfect example of peaceful co-operation amongst believing people. My prayer is that Allah's inspirations will be a comforting and motivating source for anyone seeking a confirmation.

Much appreciation is extended to all of my spiritual leaders over the years, who made my "walk" a natural progression. Special thanks for my experiences under the guidance of the late Imam Warith Deen Mohammad, may Allah forgive him and grant him paradise. His scriptural interpretation of the Bible and Quran coupled with a balanced application has been a life-changing blessing.

My dearly departed husband, Joseph E. Johnson aka Yusuf Yasin Abdullah, truly helped me in many ways on my journey to wholeness with his never-ending patience and support.

The experiences with my entire family have been the foundation from which my sentiments emanate. I am grateful that my loved ones embrace the concept of family, since creating a healthy society begins with strong families.

Special thanks to Sister Jeanette Zakkee who made this revised edition possible. Heartfelt gratitude to the believers, inside and outside of the psychiatric circle, who coached me through this thing called "life."

Peace to you all!

Ameedah

Preface

It is with deep humility that I offer this collection of writings. As a recovering mental health consumer, I feel truly blessed to be able to confess that my faith has brought me a long way. During my experiences, journaling, which I found very therapeutic, became an important part of my life. These poems were written over the past twenty eight years and represent my gratitude for the mental and spiritual growth that all of us can achieve.

It is my hope that you will find as much satisfaction with the inspirational messages as I had in preparing them. Yes, there is life after mental and emotional death when we submit to His will.

FAITH

Servitude 101	7
Time Waits For No One	8
Faith	9
Judge Not, Lest Ye Be Judged	10
Come to Prayer	11
The Declaration	12
The Debt	13
The Dandelion	14
Do You Know Him?	15
Early Morning Prayer	16
Unity In Diversity	17
Let Go and Let God	18
Song of Thanks	19
Gratitude	20
Regular Remembrance	21
The Vessel	22
Our Heritage	23
Our Obligation	24
The Love Triangle	26
Marriage 101	27
A Tribute to My Leader	28
Perceptions	30
Three Precious Ps	32

HEALING

Children of the Darkness	35
Recovery	36
Sunshine	37
Reflections On Emotions	38
The Being	39
On Self-Medication	40
A Mother's Plea	41
A Tribute to the Guardian Evolver	43
The Dream That Got Away	44
The Making of A Woman	45
In Your Time of Sorrow	46
Living For Today	47
Stigma	48

Faith

Servitude 101
1995

What can I do, Allah, to prove my love for you is true?
What can I say, Allah, to turn another head your way?
How shall I act, Allah, so everyone will see,
just how your love and mercy shines right through me?

I can thank-you in a moment or twenty-four hours a day
Always thanking you for the blessings sent my way
By trials and tribulations, you've nudged my growth
My physical and spiritual, I must acknowledge both

This overwhelming gratitude seems to fill my breast
It helps to cope with bad times, and gives the soul a rest
What can I do, Allah, to prove my love for you is true?
What can I say, Allah, to turn another head your way?

Time Waits For No One (A Song)
1981

Time waits for no one, time waits for no one,
got to be on time, cause time waits for no one

The author of time works each and everyday,
allotting lifetimes in His scientific way
When He says it's time to go,
there ain't no one who can stop the show

Time waits for no one, time waits for no one,
got to be on time, cause time waits for no one

Now you can dip and dive and joke and jive
and let your life slip by,
but it will be to late to make amends
when it's time for you to die

Time waits for no one, time waits for no one,
got to be on time, cause time waits for no one

Clean up your act, don't let your morals slack,
control your thoughts and deeds, don't let satan intercede

Time waits for no one, time waits for no one,
got to be on time, cause time waits for no one

Life is a maze, just a tunnel in time,
from one mystery to the next,
but we better hope we pass this test,
so in the end we'll all be blessed

Faith
1995

Faith is like the seed for the fulfillment of one's dreams
Faith with good intention and purpose is like the root
Faith and good deeds are like prolific foliation
By contrast, faith without purpose…
is like the seed that does not grow
Faith without good deeds …
is like the plant without soil, sun or water.
Furthermore, faith without prayer
reeks the scent of false self-sufficiency
Why not sanctify our faith by placing it in God's hands
It's like a ticket to the gates of paradise,
you can't get in without it

Judge Not, Lest Ye Be Judged
(Regarding Faith)
1995

Faith is something inward,
an intangible, an unseen,
but there are some who try to show
for the sake of being seen
It's not measured by our clothing,
outward worship, or the like
Only God can measure,
as He looks within our psyche
We must protect ourselves…
from negative judgmental thoughts
How can we decide about anything
that the Creator has brought
Our society breeds prejudice and oppression
Let's not fall victim to this obsession

Come to Prayer!!
Come to Success!!
1995

S ubmission is the key to raise humanity

U nderstanding HIS will is a blessing to achieve

C asting our desires aside, for HE knows best

C ounting our blessings, hoping to pass this test

E nvying no one, believing in our Lord

S eeking HIS mercy, spreading HIS great word

S pending of the wealth that HE bestows on us

Glorify the Creator, On Him let us put our trust!!

The Declaration (A Song)
1995

What's the first pillar of Al Islam...
without which there could be no deen?
Shahada, Shahada

To bear witness there's no God but Allah...
and Muhammad's His messenger
Shahada, Shahada

To openly declare... to know within your heart
There's no one or nothing that's worthy
of worship but Allah

It's the first pillar of Al Islam... without which
there could be no deen
Shahada, Shahada... Shahada, Shahada

To know without a doubt... Allah alone is Lord
He has no sons or partners, rely upon His word

It's the first pillar of Al Islam...
without which there could be no deen
Shahada, Shahada... Shahada, Shahada

Peace be upon Muhammad... bless his righteous soul
He told the truth of Al Quran... confirming truth of old
It's the first pillar of Al Islam...
without which there could be no deen
Shahada, Shahada... Shahada, Shahada

The Debt
1996

How do you thank the one who gave you life today?

Who fashioned you and breathed
into that mere clump of clay

Who nourished you in Mother's womb
until the time was right

Then sent you forth from darkness into the light

Mere words of thanks are not enough
to show your gratitude

But with your humble actions
and submissive attitude

To bow a head or bend a knee
and give in sincere charity

Recalling your creator in everything you do

Will show that you are grateful and He will love you

The Dandelion
1996

Do you know what delights the child,
the joy that it can bring?
The yellow flower that dots the lawn
to mark the season spring
If man knew its value,
he'd appreciate in time
One of God's most gracious gifts
it's called the dandelion

One must admit there is much pleasure
it can bring to the eye
The scene of scattered dandelions
beneath the clear blue sky
With vitamins and nutrients,
it cures ills of all kinds
It's one of God's most gracious gifts
it's called the dandelion

So let's not take for granted
or kill this so-called weed
God creates everything with value
to fulfill some valid need
Creation merely reflects His wisdom
prompting us to use our minds
A blessing from our Maker
let us learn to read His signs

Do You Know Him?
2004

Who is your Lord? Do you really know?
If you truly did, He'd show you how to go
As a fragment of His grace, He's placed you here,
To manifest His glory when we hold Him near

We each are given a job to do,
a talent, some knowledge or the like
But if we fail to use it we just abort
and walk with an empty psyche

When God creates as He wills,
He doesn't make mistakes
Submit yourself wholeheartedly,
He'll give you what it takes

The choice is ours, we must decide,
no one else can do the work
We get the things for which we strive,
be it now or in the next life

Early Morning Prayer
2008

Wake up everybody!
Call your Lord to mind
By remembering with gratitude
the peace your soul will find

You'll hear the birds at daybreak
you'll hear the rooster crow
Let's follow their example
it's something we should know

A legacy of worship, when God's angels descend
To bring His servants supplications right before Him
The static from the radio, the TV and such
Seem to always interfere with our keeping in touch

The quiet of early morning so conducive to reflect
And hear God's words of guidance
and with clarity connect
God is making His adjustments
so we must all take our place
Establishing His ways with one voice
in a united human race

Unity in Diversity
2008

Variety… the spice of life
that's the Creator's way
He creates in different species,
like the flowers that bloom in May
Each creation has its value
and procreates in its own kind
Yet when it comes to human beings
some reason with diseased minds

Human beings possess organs and systems…
to maintain their stately physique
As blood brings the air and life-giving nutrients…
truly the body is quite unique
Like flowers we have distinct features
though our bodies function the same
Like the harmony of the colors of the rainbow
after a mid-summer day's rain

Everything in the natural world
is created with a common purpose
To glorify and worship our common Creator…
by establishing His will with justice
The human is endowed with freedom
and given orders to rule this world
As believers we must reason with wisdom
as we assist the banner of truth unfurl

Let Go and Let God?
1996

Don't be filled with sadness and grief,
When your health is failing and can find no relief
Remember God's mercy, He's always been there.
He will not bestow more than you can bear
Just have faith and relax and He'll take your hand
You knew not where you came from nor where you go
But study creation and it will show,
God has His hand on every living thing
And He can renew you again, yes again
If you believe with conviction that He's ever so kind,
Be grateful and patient to achieve peace of mind

Song of Thanks
2001

When I wake up each morning, I give you all the praise
I thank you for my health and for lengthening my days
I thank you for Muhammad, my example of God's man
He taught me the wisdom to teach throughout the land
Praise be to you Allah, for making me Muslim
Glory be to you Allah, for guiding me aright
Oh, Allah, you truly are the most merciful
I truly appreciate you showing me the light
I know you're my protector, I know you are my friend
When I call on you in prayer, you give me peace within
I recognize my sins and I pray for your forgiveness
I recognize your favors, truly you're the greatest

Gratitude
2005

I am Grateful
For my tests and trials
I am grateful
In your mercy when you show me why
Therefore, I am grateful

I am grateful
For my errors
I am grateful for the truths I must acknowledge
I truly understand that you know best
Therefore, I am grateful

I am grateful
For your patience
As I wander through this life
Guiding me tolerantly, until I get it right
Therefore, I am grateful

I only pray that before my days are done
All my encounters with satan will be over and won
So I will put my trust in you and you alone
From experiences you've given me, I have truly grown
Therefore, I will always be grateful

Regular Remembrance
1996

Praise be to Allah, who wakes me daily
and gives me a sense of direction
He's taught me how to prepare for prayer
and to ask for His protection

After providing the nutrients for my body,
He sends me on my way
to finish each scheduled task with care,
seeking His pleasure today

Remembering my Lord at the noon hour
and especially in the afternoon
Will assure that my needs will be met
and blessings will come very soon.

Praise be to Allah as the day ends
and my mind becomes less cluttered
Time to read the Holy Quran
and with uncertain Arabic I will utter

Allah seems closest as the night falls
and I sense the angels nearby
When I can reflect upon His mercy
seek forgiveness and then die

The Vessel
2000

Allah gave me a vessel to live within
So that I might relate to this material place
Like a new car, it's fully loaded
With sight, hearing, smell, touch and taste

It's equipped with a voice so that I might communicate
With a wonderful brain for these features to coordinate
I guess you might say that I'm an alien on a mission
To prove my loyalty to Allah through total submission

It's important for me, in order to pass this test
To submit this vessel willingly and give my very best
I am the essence of life, without me the vessel can't live
My creation was by Allah… to Him the praise I give

When Allah calls me home and my essence departs
I pray that Allah accepts my repentant heart
He says that His grace exceeds His wrath
and on that I do depend
The Oft-Forgiving and Most Merciful
may His grace on me descend

Our Heritage
2009

Does anyone know their purpose in life?
Trying to find their destiny without any light
Through Prophet Muhammad Al Quran was revealed
Instructions for living, God's message was sealed

Allah knew this great man was ready to receive.
So Allah sent Jibril who asked Muhammad to read
Although Muhammad could not read or write,
through Allah's divine powers, he began to recite

All praise is due to Allah, each and every day
For giving life purpose and showing us the way
Upon Muhammad, I pray Allah's mercy and peace
By his excellent example, Al Islam will increase

In this month of Ramadan, when Al Quran was sent,
we ask for Allah's mercy and sincerely repent
We fast only for "His" sake, seeking "His" pleasure
For fasting is a duty only Allah can measure

Our Obligation
2009

On a blessed night in Ramadan peace abounds
For a night better than a thousand months can be found
'Twas the night Allah sent down "His" word,
by Jibril, the angel of the the Lord
To Muhammad, who received his prophetic call
to spread the truth to one and all

This encounter truly gave him a scare,
but he took up the challenge without despair
He knew that falsehood had to end,
and only on Allah could he depend
Muhammad accepted his prophetic call
to spread the truth to one and all

They called him Al Amin, the trustworthy one,
because of his honesty
Never given to idol worship,
but always reflecting on Allah's creativity
This soft-spoken, charitable man
was given this mighty role,
to warn mankind of satan
who will try to steal your soul.
Muhammad accepted his prophetic call,
to spread the truth to one and all

This was a night in Ramadan
when Al Quran was revealed
The night when the Creator said
that the prophethood was sealed
Glory to Allah for sending us instructions
with Muhammad as our guide
Let's pray to fulfill "His" plan,
as we leave our vain desires aside
Muhammad accepted his prophetic call
let US spread the truth to one and all

The Love Triangle
1983

Loving through the Creator, simply for His sake,
Is the big decision we each have to make
You're devoted to your Lord,
seeking guidance all the way
Praying that He will protect you both from going astray

As you remember Him, through your words and deeds,
He remembers you through the fulfillment of your needs
Marriage is a sacred trust, the ordained way to live
Just enjoy the blessings that the Lord will surely give

May your prayer for patience and resolve always prevail
For His promise of the "peaceful life" will never fail
Always seek his pleasure in the roles you fulfill,
For He truly loves those who submissively obey His will

Marriage 101
2009

Living and loving for the sake of Allah is truly a task
Before we commit, it's our responsibility to ask
For He knows the secrets of the unseen
Yes, He creates the love that flows in-between

We live in a society that displays an artificial love
One "they" claim we can create
But that premise creates the greatest mistakes
Often ending in broken heartache

As our spiritual consciousness expands,
as it naturally will,
Will we be able to swallow this fact
and make the love real

Sustained by the Creator
and our compliance to His will…
Will guarantee our success…
as our hearts become sealed

When we submit our will, not to each other… but to Him
Isn't it only natural that our love will win?
We must follow the truth in His Holy word
Averting divorce otherwise is simply absurd

A Tribute To My Leader Imam Warith Deen Mohammad
2008

So many qualities in our leader and teacher,
which one do we highlight?
Yet throughout his history of leadership
he would always guide to the right

He insisted on the correction of our aqeedah,
right from the very start.
The way he directed the "transition"
truly set his leadership apart.

His directive to "remake the world"
took a moment for some of us to understand
Alhamdulillah, we've caught the vision
And by Allah's grace we'll show that "We Can"

What courage as an independent thinker,
our contemporary "free man of the city"
As he defined the Medina model of peaceful co-existence,
if you can't recognize what a pity

He prepared us for the future,
by giving us the things we would need
Through his G'd-given tafsir,
he showed us how to "READ"

All praise is due to Allah
for granting us our own unique experience,
and for guiding our dearest Mujeddid,
who has made all the difference

The never-ending patience of a mother,
he catered to our every concern
Often neglecting his own desires,
so that we might learn

What sacrifice! What love!
The undeniable proof of Allah's love
Our spokesman for Human Salvation
who carried peace like the dove

Allah has given us the keys for a global renewal,
for a genesis of the human soul
We must move with enlightened vision
and hearts like the sahaba of old

It is in our hands, "We can not stop now"
all the prophets depend on us
But even more importantly, as vicegerent,
Allah has given us His trust

Perceptions
2008

Perceptions are the deterimining factor in the manner in which events unfold. You've heard that one can view the glass as half full or half empty. As always, attitude plays a major part as well. Most importantly, perceptions are our ideas or concepts that the Creator inspires in all of us as individuals. Just as He creates unique fingertips, we each have unique paths to return to our common source.

Clinicians speak of bipolar or manic-depression as malignant hyperactivity versus severe despondency and sorrow often accompanied with a desire to self destruct. However, my perception as a believer submitting to God's will, have opted to understand the experience as the manner in which the Creator chooses to utilize His servant. He has given all believers, regardless of their orientation, directives to establish the discipline necessary to fulfill His will.

Similar to the attachments on a vacuum cleaner, prayer, fasting, tithing or paying zakat or charity all work to purify our souls when attached to the belief in the Creator. All of these tools are necessary for a meaningful relationship with Him. We've heard the expression "I've got to do my spring cleaning." Spring suggests a time of renewal or new growth. It is a stage in the Creator's life cycle. Other sayings such as "Cleanliness is next to Godliness" or "Cleanliness is half of the deen" also suggests that to gain nearness to God or gain His favor, we must strive to move in that direction.

Just as we observe how God evolves His natural creation. He evolves our souls as human beings. Since we are flesh and blood, we tend to see the physical things first. Outer bodily care is necessary but does not qualify us to be utilized to our full potential. Mental or rational purification occurs when we recognize and begin to address the habits and concepts that stunt our natural growth and development. Some people might argue that what has been said is common sense. However, so many of us here, in America, have lost the common sense because we fail to use our gifts "the five senses" in a manner that would be pleasing to and approved by our Creator. Let us understand that his approval or disapproval is based on His knowledge of everything. The All-Knower in His mercy grants us a limited free will while informing us of any eminent detriment if we go against His directives. He may not spell out the consequences. Remember when our parents said, "because I said so."

Science and modern technology have been able to verify most truths that the Creator has given us long ago. In these current times, His will and directives are being manifested almost instantaneously. The Creator is the only one who can help one navigate through a spiritual evolution. Whenever He takes you to something, He will guide you through it. However we perceive our connection is there.

As a prerequisite for the afterlife, for those who believe, we must live this life with all its twists and turns. God said we must worship Him as our primary occupation in this life. Remembering the Creator in all of our endeavors, working at whatever capacity He has granted, to the best of our ability is worship. Isn't it said that "actions speak louder than words?"

In this probationary life, we are placed in various circumstances. Our attitudes and perceptions can either make us or break us. Mental illness is not God's wrath or punishment. It is a blessed test to make greater human beings.

Three Precious Ps
2009

Prayer, patience and perseverance,
concepts we must learn to master
In a world that shaitan seeks to control,
without which our lives can become a disaster
When we pray for strength to follow Allah's guidance,
we must believe His guidance is best
As we patiently wait for His will to manifest
our perseverance will help us pass each test
Islam means submission to God's will,
not necessarily what we might desire
When we follow the whispers of shaitan,
we just might end up in the fire
We must seek out peers that enjoin the right,
for shaitan undermines us through our ego
Let's trustingly line up with Allah's will
tossing our desires and then "Let Go"

Healing

Children of the Darkness
1995

Children of the darkness, from whence do you come?
Looking or searching for something or someone
Children of the darkness, from whom do you run?
Hiding in shame and trusting no one
How long can you run? How long can you hide?
When will you begin to look inside?
Childhood memories, pains of the past,
can only remain because we make them last
We must "air" our feeling, we must "air" our grief
for that is the only way to attain relief
Away with the drugs, away with the wine
accept what's inside to gain true peace of mind
We must admit that all of this medication,
would be better exchanged with "True Meditation"
Our problems and fears are out of control
Put faith in the "POWER," let anxiety unfold
I never said it would be easy,
never said you wouldn't cry,
But if you knew the relief, I know you'd surely try
GOD was there when it happened,
He knows the reasons why
Put your trust in Him, the answers will come by and by
And when the pain dissipates,
and the sun begins to shine,
thank GOD for being born again.
He is ALWAYS on time.

Recovery
2004

I can remember the days when I was so depressed
When I would get out of bed, I was really doing my best
I didn't have much to say, not even an opinion
It seemed as though life was a wakeful dream
and I was just another faceless one in it
As time passed by, and I began to look within
the naked truths were revealed
where layers of fear and guilt wore thin
Dose after dose of this and that
trying to find the magic pill to wipe away the fact
That we must learn to live on life's terms
making the best of it
If we don't accept reality we'll stay inside the pit
Once I began to trust and let my feelings flow,
'twas as if the dam had broken
and everyone should know
Now it seems I'm so excited, I want to slow back down
I've been in the air too long,
I once was lost but now I'm found
Despite the trials I've come through,
the decisions I've had to make
I pray to God daily that my spirit won't break
Just to keep the knowledge I've been given
and a chance to spread it around
To be a vehicle of positivity with my feet on the ground
Maintaining an attitude of gratitude in every situation
Taking time out each day for reverent reflection
Consulting with my Master, striving to fulfill His will
Serving mankind everyday until my flesh is still

SUNSHINE or The Bi-Polar Experience
2000

Sunshine… my favorite light
That cheers me after the stormy night
It lights the way for me to see
Exactly how I need to be
I've come this way by faith, it's true
But faith in self will see me through
Life is full of changes everyday
But with perseverance I'll find my way
New friends come and go
To shed some light to help me grow
And though the light is bright,
I must always prepare for the night
The sun will burn if I get too close
From past experiences, this I know

Reflections On Emotions
2004

An edifying observation has come to my mind,
how satan creeps into the weakest emotion he finds
He rankles and festers in your heart,
while grabbing a hold
Before we know it, we're out of control

An evil look or piercing word,
more damaging than a thrashing sword.
Knowing his tricks will keep him in check,
seeking God's help will counter this effect

Anger reeks havoc on all involved,
an outlet that must be controlled.
Fear the mental paralyzer,
prevents God's plan from being unfold

Love is something we all desire,
but if its not balanced we can land in the fire
Which of His favors will we deny?
Perhaps, when we're balanced we won't have to cry

The Being (Living In The Past)
2007

Once upon a time there was a being with a captive soul. Although the life force was present, it was unable to flow freely. The soul was encumbered as if it was stuck in a time zone like sands in an hourglass. Every time the sand flowed freely, at some point it would stop and have to retrace its steps and start over again.

This being really needed the knowledge of the "hows" and "whys" of its existence. It didn't really know who it was. Then one day God spoke directly to the soul and soon the hourglass broke. As the sands began to flow, they triggered an emotional upheaval in the being. Feelings of fear, joy, anger, guilt and relief all at once. In the hourglass captivity, the being never really had to feel emotions or direct its life in responsible decision-making. Everything was routine with no thought other than flowing from one end of the glass to the other.

With this newfound freedom, what would this soul do? Would it recognize the source of its existence and glorify its maker with gratitude and obedience? Or would it revert to the same routine it had always known out of fear or familiarity? All of us have been trapped at one time or another, but when God frees a soul, it is free indeed. So which of His favors will we deny? Will we put sunglasses on because the light of God's truth is too bright or will we embrace the light as a means to see the path and warm our spirit?

We mustn't cut off our connection with the "One" who provides for our every need. Many times when we get trapped, we lose our connection, like a short in a wire. We may feel unable to reach the source, and yet, in reality it never leaves us. Let us utilize this free spirit (soul) in service to mankind as a glorification and worship of our common source of life.

On Self-Medication
2008

We need to stop lying to ourselves…
for it is said that honesty is the best policy
We may fool some, while others we may not,
but accepting the truth is nobler than hypocrisy
Facing our fears can be frightening it's true,
but looking within is something we all must do
Many folks look outside for false contentment,
then wake up feeling sick, full of resentment

Women desire babies, maybe one or two,
without considering the pain that they will go through
God's mercy, as the "Master Surgeon,"
removes the memory as if she were a virgin
Likewise, emotional pain prevents
a naturally maturing attitude
We must trust the "Master Surgeon"
as we bask in the anesthesia of gratitude

Drugs and alcohol are an unnatural remedy
for they compound your problems, can't you see
Twelve step programs help one look within
…there's no cure for addictions until we trust Him
One can't find relief through self-medication
…but through sincere prayer and meditation
Our healing will come when we submit,
No more guilt or depression as we rise from the pit

A Mother's Plea
(On Homelessness)
2008

How will you know how much I love you,
when you never come around?
How will I ever find you,
as you wander all over town?
Will you know how much I miss you,
since you never call?
Do you ever hear the anguish in my tears as they fall?
God says not to break family ties
and to treat your parents well
Did I hurt you? Are you angry? Are you hungry?
Won't you tell?
Forever on my mind and ever in my heart,
Come back my son, can't we make a new start
Although I'm just a mother, I feel like a woman scorned
My man just up and left me
and I know not where he's gone
"Lord, protect my son and guide him to what's right"
If he doesn't care to see me,
just keep him close within my sight
Remove his mental anguish,
remind him that you reign from above
Please help him to recall how much that he is loved

In reality, I understand that he is not my son.
Lord, you are the Master of everything and everyone
I must remain steadfast in patience and prayer
God-willing he'll return
once you release him from your care
Repeatedly you've shown me that you know what is best
And although I may not understand,
I pray we'll both pass this test
I know he safely walks the streets
and you provide as well
But not knowing and letting go
has been for me a living hell
So Lord, I only ask that you supply me with the strength
to overcome my fears and guilt,
to sustain me for the full length

A Tribute To The Guardian Evolver
1995

A survivor through His Love, nourished by His Mercy
Liken to the seed that blows with the wind and
settles into the fertile soil
The stress is upon us, we sometimes deny His call
but with faith and perseverance HE will manifest it all
Praise be to the Creator
the ONLY REALITY

Come into His kingdom and set yourself free!!

The Dream That Got Away
2010

What happened to the simple things that meant so much?
What has happened to make you seem so "out of touch?"
As reflecting on God's creation once evoked great joy,
Like a child's discovery of a brand new toy
It seems as though the mysteries that used to fascinate
Have now become the primary source
to mentally frustrate
Have you been blinded by the Maker's blatant truths?
When He has provided for you a host of clear proofs
We often set our goals on the temporal things of this life
But as time passes, the realities can create internal strife
God has His way of separating the wheat from the tare
While His devotees flourish,
others seem emotionally bare.
Dreams are for sleepers who refuse to wake up
Who will not partake from the Master's cup
He offers it freely to those souls who submit
As their hopes become realities their paths become lit
Why stumble in the dark when the light is freely given?
Where we all can participate in joyful, peaceful livin'
The source that brought wonder in your youthful days
Brings greater peace as you embrace the Master's ways

The Making of a Woman
2007

Although it has been said that God first created man
We know the woman is the womb of the mind of man
It all begins when she's a child by the image she is given
By imitating mother or any other female kin
At a stage in her development, her father must step in
To validate her femininity,
she'll no longer have to pretend
After realizing her valuable role in this society,
She strives to fulfill each title to the best of her ability

As a daughter who's committed,
she aids her parents faithfully
As a sister, you can always trust her confidentiality
As a wife, she's always ready to comfort her man
She urges her husband to be the very best that he can
An important role that God enjoins on all women
either fertile or barren
Is to raise our children with the fear of God,
respect and moral livin'

The status of our women determine the state our society
We must evaluate our efforts and
strive to raise humanity
As protectors and maintainers,
men must bring the rational mind
While the woman tends to her household
and helps her husband unwind
Through God's mercy, He's given us
the model by which we should live
All praise is due to God,
it's the least that we can give

In Your Time of Sorrow
2009

Today may seem difficult, to say the least,
it seems just like yesterday
We must learn to coast along on memories
that were formed on brighter days.
And just as the sun declines at the end of each day,
without doubt, our Merciful God will again
send the radiant sun rays
He wants us to submit to His All-knowing will
With true acceptance,
we'll hear His comforting voice when we are still
In stillness, take time to reflect
on the trials that you've survived
The grateful reflections will remind you
how graced you are to be alive
Although His blessings may be disguised
in the form of calamities, by remaining faithful
His wisdom will be revealed eventually
We all are graded daily by our actions and attitudes
So we must battle with our sorrow
to maintain a thankful mood
Seize each new day to pursue your best self…
for He woke you up to serve
Steer clear of negative situations…
in which satan can throw you a curve
This life is merely a journey
and He'll travel with you all the way
Let your righteous deeds proceed you
as you make the most of each new day

Living For Today
(Blueprint For Success)
2009

One of the hardest things for some of us to do
is to appreciate the current day as a chance to start anew
It's easy to reminisce about the good or bad of the past
while the current day is wasted as it creeps away so fast
We can dream about our future,
and how good our lives will be
yet we fail to take the steps that are needed gradually.
As we reflect upon creation,
God's instructive guidebook,
we'd see that change is incremental,
if we would just look
As we plan for our contentment
in the depths of our minds
just remember when eating elephants
take one bite at a time
Our Prophet, (PBUH), said to live each day like our last
while obeying the Creator and completing every task
He also said to live as though we'll live forever
To achieve the best life we must learn to live it better
To live a purpose driven life daily gratitude is a must
Don't take today for granted for it was given as a trust

Stigma
2009

Stigma is defined as a stain or condemnation on one's reputation or as an obvious trait of defect or disease. Stigma brands one's character with shame and disgrace. These ideas constitute the reasoning why so many people who may or may not recognize that they need help are reluctant to seek counsel.

Medical science has determined that brain chemical imbalances are responsible for most of the symptoms of mental illness. Unresolved emotional issues coupled with stress are often the precipitating factors which trigger these imbalances in the human brain.

Mental illness is a lot like diabetes, however the stigma is almost non-existent for the diabetic. Just as the diabetic suffers from a chemical imbalance due to an insufficiency of insulin or an impaired ability to utilize the available insulin, the mental health consumer must also use supplemental drugs to correct the imbalance. Despite the fact that neither consumer has the option to "will away" the condition, the mental health consumer is dismissed and rejected due to the internal processes which may be inherent in his chemical make-up.

In these stressful circumstances that we face daily, we can definitely see an increase in mental conditions. We must rekindle our human compassion and seek to understand the mechanics of mental illness rather than ostracize and/or imprison those whom we can't comprehend. God has provided a number of conventional and alternative treatments to re-establish the balance and overcome these challenges.

As believers, it is our responsibility to usher in an informed awareness of mental health challenges and eradicate the barriers of stigma. We are all here as tests for one another. The human race is only as strong as its weakest links. Let us accept our oneness.

    One God, One Creation, One Humanity

ABOUT THE AUTHOR

Ameedah Diaab Abdullah, formerly known as Debra Jodi Tappan (Massey), has been a mental health consumer since 1975. Originally from New Jersey, she has been residing in Atlanta, Georgia for the last 18 years. Despite her bipolar condition, she received an associate degree in medical records and later continued her studies in psycho-social rehabilitation. She has done psychiatric peer counseling over the last several years and is currently in school working on a bachelor's degree in social work to use in the field of mental wellness.

After practicing Christianity throughout her youth, she embraced Islam via the Nation of Islam in 1974 and consequently followed the leadership of Imam W. D. Mohammad who transitioned her into mainstream Islam which is practiced worldwide.

She is also the published author of a children's book entitled *"Tell Me About Al-Islam - A Primer For Preschoolers."* She has written an article for *Azizah*, an international Muslim women's magazine, entitled *"The Beautiful Mind,"* about mental illness in the Islamic community.

She is a widow and mother of four adult children with twelve grandchildren. She is prayerful that mental wellness will become a priority in the health field.

www.ingramcontent.com/pod-product-compliance
Lightning Source LLC
LaVergne TN
LVHW051512070426
835507LV00022B/3072